Intro

Hello Rebel Queenager!

Welcome to your Happy Hormone Handbook!

I've put together this epic happy hormone, luscious lifestyle-friendly guide for you to create a healthier & happier you.

This real-life 'how to' guide will help you take action on the things you NEED to do for the results you WANT.

You know the phrase....if you do what you've always done, you'll get the results you've always had.

This guide is specifically about making simple lifestyle changes around having healthy hormone-friendly food to hand.

Alongside some proven tips that have worked for me and my 500+ clients.

So, go ahead, get stuck in. If you want to know more about me and how I can help you further check out **www.teamemw.com**

Emma x

CONTENTS

CHAPTER
01
I'm Too Busy To Meal Prep

CHAPTER
02
Happy Hormone Meal Plan & Shopping List

CHAPTER
03
Happy Hormone Recipe Pack

CHAPTER
04
The A-Z of Lifestyle Mastery

CHAPTER 01

Meal Prep

01 Meal Prep

TIME-SAVING MEAL PREP TECHNIQUES CAN SIGNIFICANTLY STREAMLINE YOUR COOKING PROCESS AND MAKE MEAL PREPPING MORE EFFICIENT. HERE ARE SOME STRATEGIES TO HELP YOU SAVE TIME IN THE KITCHEN.

MAKE IT EASY TO MAKE BETTER CHOICES AT THE END OF A PRODUCTIVE DAY.

- Batch Cooking: Prepare larger quantities of staple ingredients such as grains, proteins, and sauces on a designated day. Portion them out and use them as building blocks for various meals throughout the week

- One-Pan Meals: Choose recipes that can be cooked all in one pan. This does not only save time on cooking but also reduces the number of dishes to clean up afterward. Chiili, Curry, Spag Bol are staples, fajita's.

- Pre-Cut Vegetables and Fruits: Spend some time pre-cutting vegetables (or buy them) and fruits when you bring them home from the shop. Store them in airtight containers or bags for easy access during meal prep.

- Use Frozen and Pre-Cut Ingredients: Frozen vegetables and pre-cut ingredients like diced onions or minced garlic can be a lifesaver when you're short on time. They save you from the hassle of chopping and can be quickly incorporated into recipes.

- Slow Cooker or Instant Pot: Utilise these appliances for hands-off cooking. Prep the ingredients, set the cooking time, and let the device do the work while you attend to other tasks.

- Sheet Pan Meals: Arrange proteins and vegetables on a baking sheet, season them, and roast them all at once. This technique requires minimal preparation and cleanup.

- Mason Jar Salads: Prepare salads in mason jars by layering dressing at the bottom, followed by sturdy ingredients, and leafy greens on top. When you're ready to eat, simply shake the jar to mix the dressing and enjoy a fresh salad.

- Overnight Oats: Make breakfast prep a breeze by preparing overnight oats the night before. Combine oats, milk or yogurt, and your favorite toppings in a jar or container. By morning, they'll be ready to eat. You can make this even easier by mixing all the ingredients into a massive bowl and blending a portion every morning.

- Cooking a whole chicken/joint in the Instant Pot, will do all your lunches or 3 family dinners in roughly an hour.

- **Freezer-Friendly Meals:** Cook large batches of meals and freeze them in individual portions. You can then reheat them when needed for a quick and easy dinner.

- **Prep in Stages:** Break up meal prep into smaller tasks and spread them over a couple of days. For example, chop vegetables one day, cook proteins another day, and assemble the meals on a third day.

- **Cook Once, Eat Twice:** Prepare extra portions of dinner and use the leftovers for lunch the next day. This saves time on both cooking and meal planning.

- **Set a timer-** do as much as you can in 60/90 minutes. You can easily do 4 breakfasts/lunches & dinners for a family of 4.

By incorporating these time-saving meal prep techniques into your routine, you'll find that cooking becomes more manageable, and you have more time for other activities while still enjoying delicious and nutritious meals.

CHAPTER 02

Pro Tips

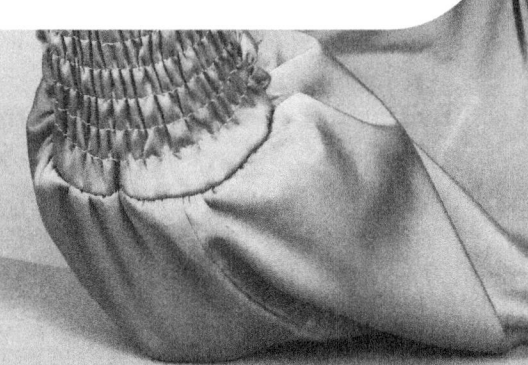

Kitchen Pro Tips

- If you've got a cupboard of chocolate 'for the kids'. Donate all of it, the rule of food is 'if it's in the house, you will eat it. If it's not, you won't. The same applies with alcohol.

- Move optimal/nutrient-dense choices to eyeline. less optimal choices go high up or low down (look at the supermarket rows on how they do this)

- Have a well-stocked cupboard & freezer, tuna, beans, micro rice, frozen steam fresh veg bags, you can rustle up a protein-rich meal in 2.5 minutes. Quicker than toast.

- Don't avoid fats. avocado, olives, oily fish, eggs, unsaturated oils. Your hormones LOVE these. A thumb-sized amount is a good portion in a meal.

- Get the family involved, chances are they are eating this too. A better education about food at an early age leads to a better relationship with food.

- On busy weeks, order pre-prepped or home delivered meals.

Kitchen Pro Tips

- Avoid decision fatigue, and make it easy to choose better. Having meals planned and prepped in advance makes it easy. If you don't you're more likely to snack or reach for the take away menu.

- Base every single meal around a protein source:
    - Breakfast: Greek Yoghurt, Eggs, and Cottage Cheese are great choices.
    - Other Meals: Lean meat, tuna, tempeh, tofu
    - Once you've decided on a protein source, then add veggies and then carbohydrates & fats.

- Challenge your 'I don't have time' excuses. A 4-day meal plan/prep can take as little as 1 hour.

- Essentials: Good knives, pans inc nonstick frying pan, quality (BPA free) containers, chopping boards.

- Useful to have: Air fryer, slow cooker, scales, someone to wash up.

CHAPTER 03

7 Day Meal Plan

Meal Plan

Brekkie	Lunch	Snack	Dinner
Spanish Courgette Tortilla	Chicken Orange & Walnut Salad	E.g. Cinnamon Roll Protein Smoothie, Protein Fruit Bowls	Chinese Pork Stir-Fry With Pineapple
Omelet Wraps	Tuna & Broccoli Salad With Honey Vinaigrette	E.g. Cinnamon Roll Protein Smoothie, Protein Fruit Bowls	Baked Salmon Tray With Rice & Tomatoes
Egg & Turkey Stuffed Peppers	Leftover Baked Salmon Tray With Rice & tomatoes	E.g. Cinnamon Roll Protein Smoothie, Protein Fruit Bowls	Beef & Green Beans Pasta In Soy Sauce
Omelet Wraps	Chicken Orange & Walnut Salad	E.g. Cinnamon Roll Protein Smoothie, Protein Fruit Bowls	Leftover Beef & Green Beans Pasta In Soy Sauce
Egg & Turkey Stuffed Peppers	Tuna & Broccoli Salad With Honey Vinaigrette	E.g. Cinnamon Roll Protein Smoothie, Protein Fruit Bowls	Waldorf Chicken Salad
Cinnamon Roll Protein Smoothie	Leftover Waldorf Chicken Salad	E.g. Cinnamon Roll Protein Smoothie, Protein Fruit Bowls	Meal Out - Enjoy!
Spanish Courgette Tortilla	Cinnamon Roll Protein	E.g. Cinnamon Roll Protein Smoothie, Protein Fruit Bowls	Chinese Pork Stir-Fry With Pineapple

Shopping List

Fruit

4 Lemons
2 Oranges
Pomegranate
2 Bananas
1 Apple
1 Mango
Strawberries

Meat & Seafood

100g Smoked salmon
400g Salmon fillet
450g Turkey Mince
300g Chicken breast
300g Beef steak
1400g Pork tenderloin

Grains & Seeds

Jasmine rice Pasta
Potato
White rice
Self raising Flour
Baking powder

Vegetables

1 Potato
3 Onions
Garlic
1 Courgette
Watercress
1 Bag spinach
1 Bag rocket
Salad leaves
Radishes

5 Bell peppers
1 Chili pepper
Ginger
1 Broccoli head
Cherry tomatoes
Celery
Spring onions

(fresh or frozen)

Dairy

Cottage cheese
Cheddar cheese
Parmesean
0% Fat Greek Yoghurt
20 Eggs
Milk

Spices

Mixed herbs
Oregano
Cumin
Cinnamon
Paprika
Curry & Chilli

Nuts & Seeds

Pecans
Walnuts
Coconut
Raisins

Herbs

Parsley
Basil

Recipes

CHAPTER 04

04

Spanish Courgette Tortilla

Ingredients
Serves 2

1 tbsp. olive oil
1 small potato, peeled
1 small onion, chopped
½ small courgette, thinly sliced
6 eggs

What you need to do

1. Heat oil in a non-stick pan and sear the potato and onion over medium-high heat, for about 4 minutes.
2. Next, add the courgette and sauté for another 4 minutes.
3. In a bowl, whisk eggs and season with salt and pepper. Transfer the vegetables from the pan into the bowl and mix well.
4. Using the same pan, add the egg mixture on low heat and make sure everything is evenly distributed. After about 3 minutes, run a spatula through the outer edges of the tortilla to make sure it does not stick to the pan.
5. After 8-10 minutes, flip the tortilla (this might take more or less, depending on heat, size and pan), using a plate over the pan. Slide the uncooked part back into the pan.
6. After another 5-6 minutes, the tortilla should be cooked. Remove from heat and serve.

GF	DF	MP	HP	V

Prep	Cook	Kcal	Fats(g)	Carbs(g)	Protein(g)
10 mins	25 mins	377	22	22	21

*Nutrition per serving

myfitnesspal

03761520

04

Omelet Wraps

Ingredients
Serves 4

7 oz. (200g) cottage cheese
4 handfuls watercress
1 lemon, peel only
6 eggs
¼ cup (60ml) soy milk
1 tsp. mixed herbs
4 tsp. coconut oil
3.5 oz. (100g) smoked salmon, chopped

What you need to do

1. Place the cottage cheese, watercress and lemon peel in a high bowl and puree with the hand blender (or food processor) until smooth paste forms.
2. Beat the eggs with the milk and herbs in a separate bowl.
3. Heat 1 tsp. of oil in the medium size frying pan and fry ¼ of the egg over medium heat for 2 minutes until the egg solidifies, then turn around. Bake the other side for ½ minute.
4. Remove the omelet from the pan and set aside.
5. Fry the other omelets with the rest of the oil.
6. To serve, spread the cottage cheese paste over the omelets and top with smoked salmon. Roll up the omelet as a wrap and cut in half.

| GF | DF | LC | Q |

Prep	Cook	Kcal	Fats(g)	Carbs(g)	Protein(g)
15 mins	10 mins	237	15	3	20

*Nutrition per serving

04

04

Egg & Turkey Stuffed Peppers

Ingredients
Serves 4

4 eggs

4 egg whites

2 tbsp. almond milk

1 tsp. coconut oil

1 small onion, chopped

1 lb. (450g) lean ground turkey

2 tsp. oregano

1 tsp. cumin

2 cups (60g) spinach, chopped

4 red medium bell peppers

½ cup (50g) cheese (dairy or plant-based)

parsley, chopped to serve

What you need to do

1. Heat oven to 400°F (200°C).
2. Beat the eggs, egg whites and milk, then set aside.
3. Heat the coconut oil in a pan over medium heat. Add the onion and cook for 3 minutes until softened and browned.
4. Add in the turkey, oregano and cumin, season with salt and pepper. Cook until meat is cooked through, about 5 minutes. Then, add the spinach, and mix until it wilts about 2 minutes.
5. Increase the heat and add in the eggs. Pull the eggs across the skillet with a spatula. Repeat for about 3 minutes until eggs are cooked. Then, set aside.
6. Cut the peppers horizontally and remove the seeds, then stuff with the scrambled eggs and turkey.
7. Place the peppers in a baking dish and sprinkle them with grated cheese.
8. Bake in the oven for 15 minutes, until cheese has melted and the edges have browned.
9. To serve, sprinkle with chopped parsley.

myfitnesspal

09361980

| GF | LC | MP | HP | Q |

Prep	Cook	Kcal	Fats(g)	Carbs(g)	Protein(g)
5 mins	20 mins	329	12	11	43

04

Chicken, Orange & Walnut Salad

Ingredients
Serves 2

For the dressing:
3 tbsp. of honey
2 tbsp. mustard
1 tbsp. olive oil
1 tbsp. lemon juice 2 tbsp. orange juice
⅓ tsp. cinnamon

For the salad:
7 oz. (200g) chicken breast
4 handfuls rocket
¼ iceberg lettuce
1 orange
⅓ pomegranate fruit, seeds
¼ cup (30g) pecans, roasted

What you need to do

1. Peel orange and cut out the pulp and set aside. Squeeze the juice from the rest of the orange and keep it for the sauce.
2. Mix the ingredients of the dressing in a cup, season with salt and pepper.
3. Cut the chicken breast into 4 smaller pieces, season with salt, coat with olive oil and place on a hot grill pan — grill for 4 minutes on both sides.
4. Drizzle the chicken pieces with a tbsp. of dressing and continue to grill for about 1.5 minutes on a slightly lower heat. Turn over then drizzle with another tbsp. of dressing, and grill for another minute.
5. Remove from the pan and set aside.
6. Once cooled slightly slice into pieces.
7. Mix the salad leaves and divide it between two plates, then top with the orange and chicken. Sprinkle with the pomegranate seeds and roasted pecans. Drizzle with the remaining dressing and serve.

GF	DF	HP	Q	N

Prep	Cook	Kcal	Fats(g)	Carbs(g)	Protein(g)
10 mins	10 mins	458	20	47	28

*Nutrition per serving

myfitnesspal
04873372

04

Tuna & Broccoli Salad With Honey Vinaigrette

Ingredients
Serves 2

For the dressing:

2 tbsp. olive oil
3 tbsp. of lemon juice 1 tsp. of honey
salt & pepper

For the salad:

2 big handfuls salad leaves
3 radishes, sliced
½ cup (120g) tuna in water, drained
2 slices bread
100g broccoli
2 tsp. Parmesan, grated

What you need to do

1. Divide the salad leaves between two plates. Add the sliced radish and pieces of tuna.
2. Toast the bread and cut into cubes, then add to the salad.
3. Place the broccoli in a pot of boiling water and cook for approx. 5 minutes, then strain and add to the salad.
4. In a bowl, mix all the dressing ingredients and drizzle over the salad. Sprinkle with parmesan cheese and serve.

	HP	Q			
Prep	Cook	Kcal	Fats(g)	Carbs(g)	Protein(g)
10 mins	0 mins	328	14	26	21

myfitnesspal

04717171

04

Waldorf Chicken Salad

Ingredients
Serves 2

3.5 oz (100g) chicken, cooked, shredded or chopped

3 celery stalks, chopped

1 apple, peeled, deseeded, chopped

¼ cup (40g) raisins

¼ cup (30g) walnuts, chopped

1 tbsp. mayonnaise

1 tbsp. natural low fat yogurt

1 tbsp. lemon juice

3 oz. (90g) mixed salad leaves

What you need to do

1. Place the chicken, chopped celery and apple, raisins, and walnuts in a bowl.
2. Add in the mayonnaise, yogurt and lemon juice, season with salt and pepper and mix well.
3. Divide the salad leaves between bowls and top with the filling.
4. Serve with freshly ground black pepper.

*Vege Option — Instead of chicken add tofu.

| GF | MP | HP | Q | N |

myfitnesspal

Prep	Cook	Kcal	Fats(g)	Carbs(g)	Protein(g)
10 mins	0 mins	354	16	33	20

Chinese Pork Stir-Fry With Pineapple

Ingredients
Serves 4

For the dressing:
14 oz. (400g) pork tenderloin
1 tbsp. potato starch
scant ½ cup (100g) white rice
⅔ cup (135ml) pineapple chucks, in juice (keep the juice)
1 red bell pepper, sliced
½ onion, sliced
2 garlic cloves
½ chili pepper
1-inch fresh ginger, grated
2 tbsp. coconut oil
2 spring onions, chopped, to serve

For the sauce:
⅓ cup (180ml) pineapple juice from can
5 tbsp. soy sauce
3 tbsp. rice vinegar

What you need to do

1. Wash the meat, pat dry, and cut them into the thinnest slices possible. Season with salt and pepper, and coat with potato flour.
2. Cook the rice according to instructions. Drain the pineapple but keep some of the juices for the sauce. Cut the peppers into strips, and the spring onions julienned. Half the chili, remove the seeds, then finely chop. Peel and grate the ginger.
3. Prepare the sauce by mixing all sauce ingredients in a bowl.
4. In a wok or large pan, heat 1 tablespoon of coconut oil, and stir fry all the vegetables (pepper, onion, garlic, chili, ginger) over high heat for about 3 minutes. Add the drained pineapple and fry together for another 2 minutes, then transfer everything onto a plate.
5. Add a second spoon of oil to the pan and fry the tenderloin on high heat for about 3 minutes, stirring constantly.
6. Put the vegetables back into the pan and mix, then add the sauce. Cook over high heat for about 2 minutes until the sauce thickens. Mix occasionally.
7. Sprinkle with chopped spring onions and serve with rice.

| GF | DF | MP |

Prep	Cook	Kcal	Fats(g)	Carbs(g)	Protein(g)
20 mins	10 mins	303	11	22	28

*Nutrition per serving

myfitnesspal

06484836

Baked Salmon Tray With Rice & Tomatoes

Ingredients
Serves 4

14 oz. (400g) salmon fillet, skin removed

1 tsp. honey

2 tbsp. soy sauce

2 tbsp. olive oil

4 slices of lemon + 2 tbsp. of juice

⅞ cup (200g) jasmine rice

1 cup (150g) cherry tomatoes

handful basil leaves

4 tbsp. natural yogurt, 0% fat

For the spices:

2 tsp. paprika

½ tsp. curry

1 tsp. oregano

pinch of chili flakes

What you need to do

1. Cut the salmon fillet into 4 pieces. Rinse, dry and place in a bowl. Season with salt, pepper, paprika, curry, and oregano. Add honey, soy sauce, 2 tbsp. of olive oil and 2 tbsp. of lemon juice. Mix everything and cover the bowl.
2. Preheat oven to 400°F (200°C).
3. Cook the rice according to the instructions on the packaging. Drain it, then transfer into a baking dish and spread the rice over the whole surface of the dish.
4. Place the salmon fillets on top of the rice, add the cherry tomatoes and basil leaves, then sprinkle with chili flakes.
5. Top salmon with lemon slices, and drizzle over the remaining marinade and bake in the preheated oven for 15 minutes.
6. Serve with a dollop of natural yogurt.

myfitnesspal

GF	MP	HP

Prep	Cook	Kcal	Fats(g)	Carbs(g)	Protein(g)
5 mins	30 mins	476	19	44	31

*Nutrition per serving

04

Beef & Green Beans Pasta In Soy Sauce

Ingredients
Serves 2

4 oz. (120g) whole-wheat pasta
10 oz. (300g) beef steak
4 spring onions
2 cloves garlic
1 tbsp. coconut oil
2 tbsp. soy sauce
⅓ cup (80ml) beef stock
100g green beans, frozen

What you need to do

1. Cook the pasta according to instructions on the packaging.
2. Cut the beef into thin slices.
3. Slice the spring onions diagonally into 1-1.5 inch pieces. Peel and slice the garlic.
4. Heat the oil in a large pan over medium-high heat and cook the beef for about 3 minutes, then transfer onto a plate and drizzle with soy sauce.
5. Add the garlic and spring onions to the same pan and cook for about 3 minutes, until spring onions start to soften.
6. Return the beef and soy sauce into the pan and add the hot stock and frozen beans. Cook for another 2-3 minutes, then add the cooked pasta. Stir occasionally for about 2 minutes.

DF	MP	HP	Q

Prep	Cook	Kcal	Fats(g)	Carbs(g)	Protein(g)
10 mins	15 mins	491	12	53	44

*Nutrition per serving

myfitnesspal

05778330

Green Glow Protein Smoothie

Ingredients
Serves 1

1 small banana
1 cup spinach
1 cup kale
1 tbsp. almond butter
⅔ cup (150ml) coconut water
1 scoop (25g) vanilla protein powder, optional

What you need to do

1. Place all ingredients into a high-speed blender and blitz until smooth.
2. Serve immediately.

Note: The protein powder is optional, but adds a boost of protein. You can use whey or any plant-based protein powder. You can also replace the protein powder with a few tablespoons of Greek yogurt (in that case reduce the amount of liquid).

| GF | HP | V | Q | N |

myfitnesspal
02539500

Prep	Cook	Kcal	Fats(g)	Carbs(g)	Protein(g)
5 mins	0 mins	350	12	34	29

*Nutrition per serving

04

Antioxidant Blueberry Protein Smoothie

Ingredients
Serves 1

½ cup (125ml) coconut water ½ cup (125ml) almond milk, unsweetened

1 scoop vanilla whey protein

½ cup (50g) frozen blueberries

1 tsp. ground cinnamon

1 tsp. chia seeds

What you need to do

1. Blend all the ingredients in a high-speed blender until smooth and serve.

GF | LC | V | Q | N

Prep	Cook	Kcal	Fats(g)	Carbs(g)	Protein(g)
5 mins	0 mins	197	4	14	26

*Nutrition per serving

myfitnesspal
06189716

04

Cinnamon Roll Protein Smoothie

Ingredients
Serves 2

1 banana
2 scoops (50g) vanilla protein powder
1 tsp. cinnamon
1 cup (240ml) almond milk
1 cup of ice cubes

What you need to do

1. Place all ingredients into a blender and pulse until smooth. Serve.

| GF | HP | V | Q | N |

Prep	Cook	Kcal	Fats(g)	Carbs(g)	Protein(g)
5 mins	0 mins	162	3	15	22

*Nutrition per serving

LIFESTYLE

CHAPTER 05

A-Z Happy Hormones

A is for:

Alcohol: Yes it's a toxin, yes it's empty calories, yes it's a depressant. No, I'm not here to tell you to cut it out, but suggest you reduce it, a bit. Your hormones don't love alcohol.

B is for:

Balanced Nutrition: That means a good mix of a single ingredient, unprocessed foods, with a few of the 'OMG you shouldn't be eating that' things thrown in. 80% of the former, 20% of the latter is a good place to be. Nutrition is the #1 tool you have for balanced hormones

C is for:

Calories Matter: Fat loss is created from being in a calorie deficit. The quality of food matters but timings of the food doesn't matter. Carrying a higher % of body fat can create too much oestrogen that then creates an 'imbalance' with other hormones.

D is for:

Daily Habits: Do you want a sustainable lifestyle change? Then you'll need to incorporate different habits. Learn to habit stack and make it as easy as possible too succeed.

E is for:

Exercise: Think of it as a tool to live longer, healthier, and age better. It's not a tool to lose weight. In fact, it's not even nearly the best thing to manage body fat. BUT, it is the best tool to create muscle mass and thats what's going to stop you from falling over and breaking bones when you're 80. So lift weights.

F is for:

Fat: Body fat and dietary fat are different things. You do not get fat from eating fat. You get fat from eating too many calories. Your hormones & brain health need dietary fat to thrive, but they need unsaturated fat. So think olives and avocados instead of cakes and crisps.

G is for:

Gratitude: What and how you think determines how you do things. If you can spend 5 minutes a day thinking of the good things in your life, you statistically have better physical and financial results in life.

H is for:

Hormones: Hormone fluctuations are normal in a womans life. Perimenopause on average lasts 15 years. Take control of the things that help hormones (like your nutrition, mindset & movement) because 'riding' it out might be a hard slog.

I is for:

Intellect: keep learning new things, it is thought that actively engaging our brain will help reduce risk of dementia and Alzheimers. Read, develop & grow.

J is for:

Joints: pay attention to your joints, strength training exercises can help support and protect your joints by strengthening the surrounding muscles. Gentle on the joints cardio based movement, such as swimming, cycling, and walking, have cardiovascular benefits too.

K is for:

Keto: Not a long-term solution for most people. When carbs are restricted most people DO see a big jump in the scales, however, this is a reduction of fluid in the cells, not a reduction in fat. Conversely the same is true, if you eat a carb-rich meal, the scales will go up. Again, this is not fat, this is fluid in the cells.

L is for:

Laughter: It's hard when you're working loads, got a family, house, and all the plates to spin. Don't forget to laugh & have fun. Laughing is so good for releasing those feel-good hormones like dopamine & seratonin

M is for:

Mindful Eating: Sometimes called intuitive eating. let's not get too fancy this is about recognising true hunger and being satisfied, not stuffed. We eat too quickly in the Western world which causes issues with gut health and over consumption of calories (causing weight gain).

N is for:

Nutrition: Nutrition, nutrition, nutrition. What you put in your body determines your health, your body composition & mood. It's he no1 thing you can do to help your hormones too. I know I have this twice. I'ts that important. you get to determine your health through the food you eat.

O is for:

Optimal Sleep: Every function in our body needs cell renewal, this happens during sleep. If you're not getting good quality or quantity (6.5hrs PLUS) sleep then nothing is going to work very well, including metabolism. Poor sleep increases cortisol levels too...skip netflix & go to bed.

P is for:

Planning: I'm too busy to meal prep (see Chapter 1)/exercise/eat healthy/sleep. Everyone's busy but other people still manage. Have a look at your planning. Are you using your calendar, are you strict with your phone time.....there's always a way to prioritise health.

Q is for:

Quick Fixes: Yes, they sound sexy & attractive. But rarely are a solution. Want to lose 2 stone in a day? On you go, but you'll gain 3 stone in a week. Put the work in over the long term and you'll get the results.

R is for:

Relaxation: Learning to switch off from time to time is a learned skill.   Self-care isn't always a spa day. It can be food and exercise. It can be 5 minutes of meditation. It can be a 30-minute walk outside. But actively try to do something! Daily if possible.

S is for:

Stress: The number one saboteur to health. Also see relaxation & sleep. Hormones can cause stress. Being unhealthy can cause stress. The workplace can cause stress. Be mindful of your levels and take action to reduce stress when you notice it.

T is for:

Tits n Teeth: Doing things that challenge us builds confidence. Unpicking beliefs that don't serve us, creates a new future. Creating new goals and understanding WHY we want those things is. agamechanger. And doing those things requires those shoulders back, those tits out and a big grin.

U is for:

Understanding: You are not 32. What worked for you then, will not work for you now. Being all or nothing with your food and exercise, used to be a great tactic to lose a stone, now it's going to be an impossible task. You are not superwoman (or a martyr) use other people to help you get shiz done.

V is for:

Vitality & Va Va Voom: Hormones might make you sluggish, poor nutrition might make you sluggish too, so might dehydration. Want more energy, look at the things you can control before relying on supplements, caffeine or sugar.

W is for:

Water: Drink more. Seriously, dehydration causes poor mental engagement, low physical energy, fatigue, hunger.......aim for 2-3 litres a day. And be consistent, so that the peeing settles down (takes about a week)

X is for:

The Ex Version Of You: Want to feel like your old self? You can, OR, you get to create a new version of you, That's eXciting isn't it?

Y is for:

Yoga: stretching or mobility work is a fundamental principle of movement. Have you heard the phrase- motion is lotion? Use those joints and muscles, or lose the. You can see huge benefits in your mobility in just 5 minutes a day.

Z is for:

Zero comparisons: Comparison is the thief of joy. There is always going to be someone fitter, leaner, richer, prettier, taller, shorter, smarter than you. Learning to love and challenge yourself is the ultimate in self-care and compassion.

About

Meet Emma McElhinney (Mack-El-Hine-Knee), Founder Team EMW, Rebel Queenager & Fun lover

As a trailblazing perimeno & behaviour change specialist, Emma's mission is to transform women who feel marooned in monotony into their audacious, dazzling, ultimate badass selves.

Emma's flagship powerhouse, The Happy Body Project, has steered over 500 women from feeling stuck in their old dress sizes to rocking hot AF body transformations alongside sustainable lifestyle and behaviour makeovers.

Her work has graced the pages of Lift The Bar fitness magazine, The Sun Newspaper, Boots Health Magazine, The i Newspaper and Saga.

Fuelled by an unquenchable passion for personal development and a drive to help women morph into their most fabulous selves,

Emma's got a knack for delivering straight talk intertwined with a healthy dose of cheesy motivational nuggets. So buckle up!

What to do now, contact me TODAY!

www.teamemw.com

Printed in Great Britain
by Amazon